Michelle Obama

FIRST LADY

by Meg Gaertner

FOCUS
READERS.

BEACON

www.focusreaders.com

Focus Readers is distributed by North Star Editions:
sales@northstareditions.com | 888-417-0195

Produced for Focus Readers by Red Line Editorial.

Photographs ©: Paul R. Giunta/Invision/AP Images, cover, 1; Carolyn Kaster/AP Images, 4; David Goldman/AP Images, 6; Shutterstock Images, 8, 13, 20–21, 25, 27; John Gress/Reuters/Newscom, 11; Dan Cross/Sipa/AP Images, 14, 29; WDC Photos/Alamy, 16; Wong Maye-E/AP Images, 19; Olivier Douliery/Sipa/AP Images, 22

Library of Congress Cataloging-in-Publication Data
Library of Congress Cataloging-in-Publication Data is available on the Library of Congress website.

ISBN
978-1-64493-690-0 (hardcover)
978-1-64493-726-6 (paperback)
978-1-64493-798-3 (ebook pdf)
978-1-64493-762-4 (hosted ebook)

Printed in the United States of America
Mankato, MN
012021

About the Author

Meg Gaertner is a children's book editor and writer. She lives in Minneapolis, where she enjoys swing dancing and spending time outside. She is grateful for the opportunities she has, and for the important women whose groundbreaking work made those opportunities possible.

Table of Contents

Chapter 1

Reach Higher

In 2014, First Lady Michelle Obama spoke to students at a high school. She talked about her childhood. Her parents hadn't gone to college. But Obama had wanted to go to Princeton University.

 Michelle Obama speaks to students at Wayne State University in 2015.

 At a college fair in 2014, students learn about different options for higher education.

So, she made it happen. She took control of her future. Obama told students they could do that, too.

Obama started the Reach Higher program. It encouraged students to continue schooling after high school. It helped them understand their options. Students can attend college. They can also get training.

Obama believes higher education helps people succeed. She has supported other causes, too. She has been a leader in and out of the White House.

Did You Know?

Reach Higher taught students about job opportunities. It helped them get money to go to college.

Chapter 2

Born to Lead

Michelle LaVaughn Robinson was born on January 17, 1964. She grew up in Chicago, Illinois. Her mother was a stay-at-home mom. Her dad worked in a water treatment plant.

Michelle grew up on the South Side of Chicago.

Robinson left Chicago after high school. She went to Princeton University. Then she studied at Harvard Law School.

After graduating, Robinson returned to Chicago. She worked at a law firm. There, she met Barack Obama. She married him in 1992.

Did You Know?

Michelle's dad worked hard at his job. He inspired her. She works hard because of his example.

 Michelle and Barack Obama had two daughters, Sasha (left) and Malia.

She took his last name and became Michelle Obama.

Obama decided to focus on **public service**. She worked for the city of Chicago. She also formed the Chicago branch of Public Allies.

Public Allies is a program for young people. It trains them to be leaders in their communities. Obama served as the branch's director from 1993 to 1996.

Obama worked for the University of Chicago next. She helped bring the school and the community together. She also helped students be more involved in the community. She encouraged them to **volunteer**.

Obama's husband ran for president in the 2008 election.

Obama gives a speech during her husband's campaign for president in 2008.

Obama left her job to help with Barack's **campaign**. She talked to voters. Her help made a difference. Barack won the election. He took office in 2009.

Chapter 3

First Lady

Michelle Obama was the first Black First Lady. She was First Lady from 2009 to 2017. During this time, she started four key programs.

Let's Move began in 2010. Its goal was to end childhood **obesity**.

 As First Lady, Obama knew the world was watching her words and actions.

 Obama runs with kids during a Let's Move event in July 2012.

Obama worked with officials and community leaders. Together, they made sure schools offered healthy food. They brought healthy food to **underserved** communities. They educated parents about keeping kids healthy. And they helped kids be more active.

In 2011, Obama formed Joining Forces. This program supported members and **veterans** of the US military. **Service members** help protect Americans. They travel and work to keep US citizens safe.

Did You Know?

Obama planted a vegetable garden on the White House lawn. She shared the food with the local community.

But when they come home, they often face hard times. They may struggle to find jobs. Some become homeless. Many face health issues.

Joining Forces helped veterans. It tried to make sure they got health care. It connected them to training programs. Joining Forces also helped them find jobs.

Did You Know?

In five years, Joining Forces helped more than one million people get jobs.

 Obama visits a high school in Cambodia in 2015.

In 2014, Obama started Reach Higher. This program promoted higher education in the United States. In 2015, she started Let Girls Learn. It helped girls around the world receive an education.

Let Girls Learn

Obama believes in **empowering** young people, especially girls. But millions of girls worldwide are unable to go to school. So, Obama created Let Girls Learn. It looked at the barriers keeping girls from school. For example, some girls have poor health. Or they are not safe in their homes. Other girls are not taught the importance of education.

Let Girls Learn worked to remove these barriers. It worked with countries around the world. Volunteers trained teachers to better support girls. They helped girls stay healthy and safe. And they trained girls to be leaders.

Educators are working to help more girls pursue careers in math and science.

Future
of
Space craft

Chapter 4

Beyond the White House

Obama left the White House in 2017. She took some time off to rest. But she soon made plans to continue her work. Obama knows many people listen to her. They care about what she has to say.

Obama's influence didn't end with her time in the White House.

So, she speaks to people about important causes. She asks people to take action.

In 2018, Obama started the Girls Opportunity Alliance. This program works on education. Its goal is to educate the millions of girls who have not finished high school. People all around the world are working toward this goal. Obama's program helps connect them. It gives them tools. And it gives money to their projects.

 Obama encourages people to vote, even in small, local elections.

Obama also helped start When We All Vote. This program works to get people registered to vote. It asks all Americans to vote. Obama believes that voting is how citizens make sure their concerns are heard.

Voting shows what causes and ideas people care about. That way, lawmakers can make changes.

Throughout her life, Obama has supported many causes. She has encouraged young people to make healthy choices and get higher education. She has helped service

 Obama called her memoir *Becoming*. This title reflects her work and hope for change.

members. And she has promoted girls' education.

Obama continues to serve the public in many ways. She keeps working to make change. Plus, she asks others to join her.

FOCUS ON
Michelle Obama

Write your answers on a separate piece of paper.

1. Write a sentence summarizing the main idea of Chapter 3.

2. Which of the four programs that Obama started as First Lady do you think is most important? Why?

3. When did Obama start Let Girls Learn?
   A. 2010
   B. 2014
   C. 2015

4. How did Obama's public service in Chicago help her as First Lady?
   A. It prepared her to be a leader on key issues.
   B. It helped her study harder in school.
   C. It helped her husband become president.

5. What does **programs** mean in this book?

During this time, she started four key programs. Let's Move began in 2010. Its goal was to end childhood obesity.

    A. lists of the songs in a concert

    B. sets of activities with long-term goals

    C. groups of people that play a game

6. What does **barriers** mean in this book?

It looked at the barriers keeping girls from school. For example, some girls have poor health.

    A. things that keep people from doing something

    B. things that block people's vision

    C. things that allow people to do something

Answer key on page 32.

Glossary

campaign
A series of activities to convince people to vote for a certain person.

empowering
Helping people to feel like they can do something.

memoir
A book or essay that tells about a person's life and memories.

obesity
The condition of being severely overweight.

public service
Jobs that aim to serve all members of a community.

service members
People who are part of the armed forces, such as the army, navy, marines, air force, or coast guard.

underserved
Not having access to the same services and resources as other areas.

veterans
People who have served in the military.

volunteer
To help out without being paid.

To Learn More

BOOKS

Corey, Shana. *Michelle Obama: First Lady, Going Higher.* New York: Random House, 2018.

Schwartz, Heather E. *Michelle Obama: Political Icon.* Minneapolis: Lerner Publications, 2021.

Wilson, Lakita. *Michelle Obama: Get to Know the Influential First Lady and Education Advocate.* North Mankato, MN: Capstone Press, 2020.

NOTE TO EDUCATORS

Visit **www.focusreaders.com** to find lesson plans, activities, links, and other resources related to this title.

Index

Answer Key: 1. Answers will vary; **2.** Answers will vary; **3.** C; **4.** A; **5.** B; **6.** A